Chameleons

Chameleons

ON LOCATION

KATHY DARLING

PHOTOGRAPHS BY TARA DARLING

LOTHROP, LEE & SHEPARD BOOKS   NEW YORK

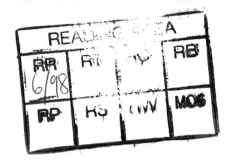

ACKNOWLEDGMENTS

We would like to thank Dr. Gary W. Ferguson, Professor of Biology at Texas Christian University, Ft. Worth, Texas, for reading this manuscript for factual accuracy and for sharing chameleon knowledge that helped us immensely on our four expeditions to Madagascar.

Library of Congress Cataloging in Publication Data Darling, Kathy. Chameleons: On location / by Kathy Darling; photographs by Tara Darling.   p.   cm. ISBN 0-688-12537-9. — ISBN 0-688-12538-7 (lib. bdg.) 1. Chameleons—Juvenile literature. 2. Chameleons—Madagascar—Juvenile literature. [1. Chameleons.] I. Darling, Tara. ill. II. Title. III. Series: Darling, Kathy. On location. QL666.L23D37   1995   597.95— dc20   94-14584 CIP AC

Contents

Green means "I feel good" to many different kinds of chameleons. This is a parsonii, the heaviest of all 128 species.

It's Not Easy **1** Being Green

If you were a pardalis chameleon, you could change the color of your skin. In just seconds, you could turn a white coat into a yellow one, decorate yourself with blue stripes, or make dozens of little orange polka dots appear and disappear. You could create all the colors in the rainbow, but you'd probably want to be green.

Skin color doesn't reveal many things about people, but it tells a lot about chameleons. They "talk" in a language based on skin colors and patterns. Chameleons flash a lot of skin messages, but they are always about the same thing: how the message sender is feeling. A black skin means a pardalis is angry or cold. One with tan coloring is sleepy. And in the language of chameleons, green skin means something

like "I am a calm and peaceful lizard."

It's not easy being green. That's because chameleons have terrible tempers. When a lizard loses its temper, it loses its calm green color, too. A chameleon can't control its color changes any more than you can keep from turning red when you feel embarrassed.

Problem is, pardalis and other rain-forest chameleons *need* to be green. Green skin is like a camouflage jacket. Without protective coloration, the slow-moving lizards can't hide from their enemies. But important as it is to hide, the short-tempered chameleons often get so excited, they break cover.

Although most people know about the chameleon's ability to change colors quickly, they are surprised to discover that the lizards can't use the speedy switches to

Minima chameleons are not good color changers.

camouflage themselves. Chameleons have two different systems for altering colors, one fast, the other slow. Changing color for camouflage—to match their surroundings—is always done with the slow system. This kind of transformation, shared by the other color-changing lizards, takes many minutes or even hours. It is controlled by chemicals called hormones, which send messages in the blood. All the pigment cells receive the same message, so animals whose color-changing instructions are delivered by hormones cannot make spots or dots or any other patterns. Only solid colors are possible.

The nervous system, like a computer, is powered by electricity. It's a much faster way of transmitting information. With this method, the entire skin can be recolored in less than 15 seconds. Each of a chameleon's millions of pigment-bearing cells is connected to a separate nerve. And because the speedy system can deliver a *different* set of instructions to each cell, patterns and designs can be produced.

The mysterious color-coded skin messages are a complicated language that is poorly understood by human observers. Even baby chameleons find it difficult. It takes about a year of practice before a student chameleon can "read" and "write" in the "language" of its kind.

Even with practice, not every chameleon can produce the pardalis's rainbow of colors. Some species are born with more color-changing ability than others. These are the mean ones! It seems that the more

This parsonii is black with rage.

spectacular the color changes, the grumpier the chameleon. Pardalis rank at the top in both departments.

"Chameleon" means "little lion," and the courageous reptiles live up to the name. They are fearless fighters. The size of an opponent doesn't seem to matter. If cornered, a three-pound pardalis will attack a human. One of the males we studied not only attacked us, he challenged *airplanes* every time they flew over his territory.

Chameleon translators don't always believe what the colors say. Sometimes chameleons don't tell the truth. Scientists call their little deceptions disinformation.

If a chameleon is detected by an enemy, it may tell a colorful "lie" to save itself. Using its brightest skin shades, the chameleon makes itself as visible as possible. This daring move is meant to confuse the enemy. Bright coloring is usually associated with poisonous animals, but since chameleons are not known to be venomous, this is probably disinformation.

The basic ingredient of quick color changes—whether used by chameleons, frogs, fish, or octopuses—is the same: a pigment cell filled with melanin. This dark pigment is responsible for all black, brown, and gray coloring in the animal world. Melanin can also work with other pigments to produce red or yellow, as it does in chameleons and humans.

Melanin alone isn't the secret of a rainbow skin. Four of the chameleon's five skin layers play a part in the production of the shifting colors.

This balteatus chameleon wants you to think he has big teeth, but it's disinformation.

LAYER 1—the deepest layer, contains melanophores: the cells that hold the dark pigment. Melanophores look like an upside-down root system that extends up through the bottom four layers of skin. The size and shape of these cells never vary. Pigment moving inside them produces most of the color changes.

LAYER 2—is a reflector layer that can look white. This layer is colorless, but its regularly shaped cells, called iridocytes, reflect white.

LAYER 3—is a reflective layer that can appear blue. Its cells, which have no pigments, contain chemical crystals called guanine. If there is light pigment under the guanine, the layer appears colorless. If there is dark pigment beneath it, the guanine cells refract (bend) blue light and the layer appears blue.

LAYER 4—has two types of cells. The large ones contain red or yellow pigment. The small cells contain droplets of yellow oil. The oil acts as a filter, giving a yellow tint to the color cells beneath them. If layer three is blue, then the yellow filter makes the skin appear green.

LAYER 5—the top layer, is clear. None of the color-changing mechanisms are found here, and this part of the skin is shed regularly.

CROSS SECTION OF CHAMELEON SKIN

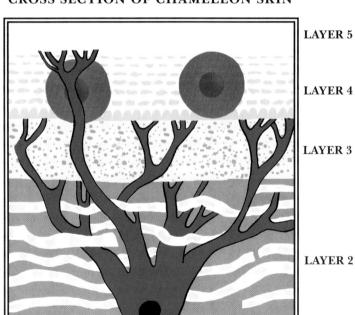

LAYER 5

LAYER 4

LAYER 3

LAYER 2

LAYER 1

Charlotte Hommey

The colorful pardalis makes good use of all five layers of its skin.

The top layer is watertight and is formed of a protein called keratin, the same tough material from which our skin, hair, and fingernails are made. The chameleon's lumpy, bumpy scales are simply thick folds of this layer.

Tara and I had the good luck to see what may be the strangest combat in the animal

A cowardly parsonii tries to slip away into the rain forest.

kingdom—a chameleon color war. In color wars, the fighters don't make a sound or move a muscle. All the action is in the skin. Battles are fought with messages written in color. First there are threats exaggerating physical abilities. They proclaim how strong and healthy the message sender is. His opponent comes back with threats of its own.

At this point, unless one of the fighters is willing to surrender, color wars turn into serious fights with lots of biting, scratching, and bleeding. Yellow skin is the surrender signal in many chameleon species. You may have heard the expression "yellow coward." It refers to chameleon fighting.

Changing skin color isn't easy. Moving

pigments takes a lot of energy. At night, when it is necessary to conserve energy, the dark pigment settles in the deepest layer of skin. A sleeping pardalis is usually a light tan produced by gray melanin and the overlying yellow filter of layer four. A sick or tired chameleon reveals its condition with an energy-saving pale brown color.

Reptiles are not generally thought to have feelings and emotions. But, with their color talk, chameleons have shown us that they do. If we learn to read them, the skin designs of these cold-blooded animals will let us know many of their secret thoughts.

HOW TO "READ" CHAMELEON

 Green = calm and peaceful

 Bright stripes = angry

 Tan = sleepy, cold, tired, or sick

 Black = REALLY angry

 Yellow = surrender

 Black with orange dots = pregnant

Both sexes can change colors, but males are usually more brightly colored and have a greater variety of color changes than females. Baby chameleons are light brown or green until they learn to "read." This chart shows pardalis chameleons.

Reptiles from Hell 2

To study chameleons, Tara and I went to an ideal location—a place called Hell. This town in Madagascar would also be the perfect place to make a horror movie with prehistoric monsters. Chameleons, as scary looking as any dragon, cruise through the trees in town and lurk in the thick greenery of the nearby jungle. With a little imagination, you could cast these mini-monsters as baby dinosaurs.

It is not surprising that chameleons remind us of dinosaurs. Both belong to a group of animals called reptiles. Millions of years ago, reptiles were the dominant form of life on Earth. The dinosaurs are all extinct now, and the rest of the reptiles are vastly reduced in both variety and number. The 6,000 modern reptile species, some almost identical to animals that lived alongside the dinosaurs, have been divided into four groups: 1) turtles and tortoises, 2) alligators and crocodiles, 3) the tuatara (an ancient lizardlike creature), and 4) lizards and snakes. Like all related groups, they have many things in common. Reptiles all have bones. They all breathe air, depend on outside sources for body heat, and have a scaly skin. Most of them lay eggs.

Chameleons are a group of lizards that are specialized for a life in the trees. Fifty-three of the 128 known species live only on Madagascar, a huge tropical island off the southeast coast of Africa. The rest hide out in Africa and some of the surrounding areas. None can be found on the American continents, in Australia, or in Asia east of India.

More than half of all reptiles are lizards, like this male lateralis chameleon.

A male parsonii, or sloth chameleon.

pardalis are the most colorful. They are able to live in the same rain forest because each uses a different part of it.

Parsonii live high in the trees. The males are the heaviest of all chameleons and are often over two feet long. They're nicknamed "sloth chameleons" because they are slow—even by chameleon standards. Parsonii eat

A male pardalis chameleon, which the Malagasy call "panther."

Another reason we chose to go to Hell was because it is surrounded by one of the most endangered rain forests on Earth. Eighty-five percent of Madagascar's beautiful forests are *already* gone. They are disappearing faster than those of the Amazon or Africa. Although there are only three different species of chameleons in the rain forest around Hell, those three are very special. Parsonii are the world's biggest chameleons, minima are the smallest, and

A male minima, or stumptail chameleon.

insects, the normal diet of chameleons, but their great size enables them to also capture and eat small birds, mammals, and lizards.

The pardalis (which means "spotted lion" or "leopard") is called "panther" in Malagasy, the native language of Madagascar. It is surviving better than most species because of its preference for bushes and small trees. Pardalis can adapt to places where the forest has been cleared, and they are often seen hunting around the edges of sugarcane fields or in the pepper farms around Hell.

The minima is a stumptail chameleon. Barely over an inch in length, it is not only the smallest chameleon, it is thought to be the world's smallest land animal with bones. Stumptails are not very colorful chameleons, and the members of this group don't climb very well. Their short lives are spent disguised as dead leaves on the forest floor.

The flat shape and ragged outline of climbing chameleons is leaflike, too. Their disguise goes beyond looking like part of the trees. Before moving, they wait for a

Temper tantrum: this male pardalis is all puffed up with anger.

breeze; then they set off in a swaying walk that looks just like a leaf blowing in the wind. A leaf-shaped body assists with heat control, too. During the hottest part of the day, when the sun is directly overhead, the narrowness of a chameleon's back provides protection from overheating. Early and late in the day, when a chameleon needs to absorb heat, the sun's rays strike its big flat sides. This strange shape centers all the weight directly above the feet. This enables a chameleon to balance on the narrowest of twigs.

Another adaptation for climbing is an unusual shoulder assembly. The shoulder blades pivot forward with the legs, adding extra inches to the chameleon's reach.

Chameleon feet, with their sharp claws, are made for gripping trees. The toes, which seem to spring right out of the ankles, are divided into two bundles that form a V. Each front foot has a bundle of two toes on the outside and a bundle of three on the inside. This arrangement is reversed on the hind feet, for added strength. A chameleon's grip is so strong that you would have to break its legs or pry open its feet to get it off a branch. The V-shaped feet grip even when a chameleon sleeps.

With their tails wound into a flat coil for added balance, chameleons sleep standing on a branch. They have favorite sleeping spots and return to them night after night. If the branch is disturbed, a sleeping chameleon automatically lets go and drops to the ground, where it has a better chance to escape from night hunters.

Leaping from trees isn't as dangerous as it sounds. Chameleons have a built-in parachute—lungs with fingerlike projections that can rapidly inflate the body. A falling chameleon instantly blows itself up like a big balloon. When it hits something, the inflated chameleon bounces. If it falls into water, it usually floats.

A chameleon's tail is prehensile. That means it can grip things. Chameleons, except for the stumptail group, can hang

upside down, supported only by the tail. As it climbs through the trees, a chameleon uses its tail as a fifth foot when the going gets tricky. A narrow body makes it difficult for a chameleon to walk on the ground without tipping over, but its long tail, stuck straight out behind, acts as a balancing rod. Unlike most lizards' tails, which can be broken off as an escape mechanism and then regrown, a chameleon's tail is not replaceable. A wild chameleon without a tail rarely survives.

"Run" isn't a word you would use to describe chameleon movement. They don't dart from place to place like other lizards, which can be ten times as fast. Chameleons live life at a slow pace. For most of the day and all of the night, chameleons stand motionless on a perch. When they do move, they move slowly.

Moving slowly or not at all is one way a chameleon saves energy. The slower it moves, the less food it needs to eat. Reptiles can survive on only ten percent of the food

A firm tailhold saved this pardalis from a nasty fall.

a mammal of the same size would require. This enables them to live in places where other animals can't make a living. And it greatly increases their chances for survival.

Reptiles are called cold-blooded, but in fact the body temperature of chameleons is about the same as ours. It is controlled differently, though. A mammal or bird keeps its body warm by burning food. Reptiles do it in a more efficient way by moving in and out of the sun. The reptile method of temperature regulation is an excellent way to warm up, but it's not very good at controlling overheating. The waterproof skin of a reptile has no rapid cooling device comparable to sweat glands in mammals.

Heat-stressed chameleons often die. Many of the animals captured for pets die of overheating during transport. Chameleons do not handle stress of *any* sort well. In the wild, they try to avoid excitement. They live alone, remain in familiar surroundings, and keep to a daily schedule.

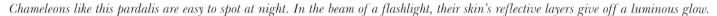

Chameleons like this pardalis are easy to spot at night. In the beam of a flashlight, their skin's reflective layers give off a luminous glow.

There is a big difference between male and female chameleons. Males are more colorful, and their colors are brightest in mating season (December–March), as can be seen from this pardalis courting couple.

Read My 3 Lipstick

The male pardalis was on the move. With speed that began to approach that of a turtle (half a mile an hour), he swayed through the bush outside our window. The cause of his unusual haste was another chameleon in his territory. Pardalis chameleons don't allow trespassers. The angry landlord, puffed up to twice his normal size to frighten the enemy, was "dressed to kill." His fighting colors included a bright yellow outline around the mouth.

Tara and I smiled. To us, it looked like he was wearing yellow lipstick. It wasn't meant to be funny, though. It was a warning to other male pardalis, as clear as a KEEP OUT sign would be to you. However, the trespasser was a *female* pardalis. To her, the yellow lips had a different meaning. They were an invitation to mate.

She quickly flashed a color-coded message identifying herself as a female ready to mate.

She was still nervous—and for good reason. The bigger, stronger males sometimes hurt the females during mating. This male's approach to breeding was simple but violent: grab the female, hold her down, and mate before she escapes.

Not surprisingly, the female didn't like to be held down. All during the forty-five-minute mating outside our window, the female struggled to get away. But the male pinned her down, biting and scratching her till blood flowed. Violence is not always the case in chameleon mating, but it happens.

The Malagasy people call a female chameleon that is about to lay eggs, like this pardalis, kamara.

A few weeks later, the female made a rare trip to the ground. She was wearing the pardalis "maternity dress" of black skin dotted with orange patches, but even without it, we would have guessed she was pregnant. Half her body weight was eggs, and the lumpy outlines were clearly visible under her scaly skin. It was obviously time to dig a nest.

She selected a spot in the damp leaf litter of the rain-forest floor and began to scratch a hole with the sharp claws of her front feet. It was dangerous for her on the ground, but she dug for hours, passing the dirt from front feet to back. All we could see was her tail and the dirt coming out. The dirt was not exactly flying. Chameleons don't dig any faster than they walk. Both activities have all the action of a slow-motion movie. After ten hours of steady work, the hole was only eight inches deep.

Eight inches was apparently deep enough, for she turned and slowly backed into her nest hole. It was easy to tell when she began to lay. Her body shook as she squeezed each of the thirty rubbery white eggs from her body. When the whole clutch was safely deposited, she scratched dirt back into the hole, circling the nest, carefully patting everything smooth with her feet, her elbows, and sometimes even her nose. It was almost dark when all signs of the digging were hidden and the tired and much slimmer pardalis made her weary way onto a night perch. Her responsibilities as a parent were over and she would not return to the nest.

This was not her only nest. She mated several more times and laid additional clutches of eggs, each in a different spot, over a period of four or five months. Surprisingly, all 150 eggs hatched at about the same time.

It takes from 180 to 300 days for pardalis babies to develop inside the eggs. Nobody can predict exactly how many days it will take for eggs to hatch because the babies can do something remarkable. They can stop growing and wait if conditions

Chameleon eggs need no camouflage colors, since they are buried immediately after they are laid.

aren't right for them to be born. With this special ability, called diapause, many kinds of chameleon embryos can stay inside their eggs even when they are ready to hatch. If the soil is too dry and hard for them to tunnel through, the little chameleons will wait. After the rain comes, the babies burst into the sunlight together on their shared birthday.

All the food a chameleon embryo needs

is inside the shell. The large golden yolk of concentrated food is connected directly to the embryo's digestive system. Waste products are collected in a sort of garbage bag connected to the baby's rear end. When the young reptile leaves the egg, it also leaves behind these stored wastes. An animal in an eggshell cannot dispose of its poisonous wastes in liquid form as mammals do. Urine would drown it. So it combines all its wastes into a white semisolid substance that requires very little water to carry it off. Many birds, reptiles, and other egg-born creatures use this system throughout their lives.

You might wonder how developing chameleons breathe inside their eggshells. Even though the eggs are buried, it's not a problem. They can breathe right though the shell. There are thousands of little holes in the shell called pores, which let oxygen in and carbon dioxide wastes out. Water gets in and out too, so the nesting place must be very carefully chosen. Developing lizards must absorb the water they need from the moist soil around the nest. If the nest isn't damp enough, the eggs overheat and cook, or they dry out and the babies die of thirst. Too much water can be just as bad. Chameleons can drown in the egg. Or fungus can grow on the shell and rot the embryo inside. One rotten egg can spoil the whole clutch. The rotting fungus can spread to other eggs, and its smell can also attract ants, snakes, and other predators. Although a number of chameleon embryos die, the majority make it to hatching time.

No chameleon parent waits nearby to encourage or protect the little lizards as they climb out of the ground. Parental care of babies is not known among lizards. No matter. Nature has prepared little chameleons to make their way alone in the world. Anything they don't already know, they teach themselves.

The hunt for food begins almost immediately. Of course, being only three quarters of an inch long, a newborn chameleon needs something small for its

This baby pardalis will not let go with its back legs until it has a sure grip with its front legs.

first meal. Fortunately there are plenty of bite-sized fruit flies and mosquitoes in Madagascar's rain forests.

Tara and I couldn't tell the male and female hatchlings apart. Both sexes are the same size and color, and the reproductive organs are internal. For the first six months all the young chameleons have the brown coloring of females. Then, suddenly, the males are able to make their adult colors, and the forest fills with flashing rainbows as they challenge one another for territory.

Zap! The cockroach doesn't stand a chance. It's fast food for this hungry hunter, which captures it in less than a second.

Sharpshooters 4

Chameleons are the sharpshooters of the animal world. They earned the title with a rather unusual weapon: their tongues. They are lightning fast and death to insects. In months of watching, Tara and I rarely saw a chameleon miss a meal.

Any insect that creeps, crawls, or flies in the rain forest is in danger when a chameleon is hunting. Although they have favorite foods, chameleons will eat grasshoppers, butterflies, caterpillars, mosquitoes, and even Madagascar's giant hissing cockroaches.

When food is within shooting distance, the chameleon opens its jaws slightly, as if it were about to yawn, and a club-shaped knob appears in its mouth. The muscular tip of the chameleon's tongue, looking a lot like a wad of bubble gum, slowly slides forward till it is sticking out two or three inches. For several seconds, the chameleon rocks from side to side, calculating aim and range with its bulging eyes. Then—*zap!*—the long tongue shoots out and hits the insect at high speed. Aided by sticky mucus, the end of the tongue forms a suction cup, much like the projectile from a toy dart gun, that attaches to the body of the insect. Before the bug knows what is happening, the chameleon has reeled in its helpless victim.

The action is too fast for the human eye to follow, but slow-motion movies reveal what happens. The chameleon's amazing tongue extends to one and a half times its body length in a sixteenth of a second. In another quarter of a second it is neatly repacked in the mouth.

Although a chameleon can pull half its body weight with its tongue, if the target is large, the chameleon often walks forward, gathering the tongue into its mouth as it advances. If the long tongue should become tangled in the branches or hit the wrong target, the chameleon can release the suction hold immediately.

Obviously, this weapon works best in aerial operations. The tongue, when extended, is limp. The heavy tip hangs down just as a weight attached to a rubber band would. If chameleons had to hunt on the ground, the wet tip would be covered with dirt after each shot. The tiny stumptails, which do hunt on the ground, have gotten around the problem. They have a shorter tongue and are able to pull it back before it hits the dirt.

There is no tongue in the world like the chameleon's high-speed missile. When it is not in use, the enormous tongue lies deep in the throat. If prey is sighted, a V-shaped bone moves the tongue into firing position in the mouth.

The tongue is a hollow tube of muscles and ligaments that slides over a slim spike of bone and cartilage called the hyoid. The tube is over forty times as long as the hyoid and is scrunched up on it like a sleeve pushed up your arm. The tip of the tongue is a knob made of donut-shaped muscles called accelerators, which tighten around the hyoid. While these muscles are squeezing, other muscles called retractors hold the rest of the tongue in its pleated position. When the chameleon decides the time is right for a shot, the retractor muscles are suddenly released. Then the donut-shaped muscles have nothing to resist them, and the tongue jets off the end of the hyoid.

The tongue is deadly because it is aimed accurately. Chameleon eyes, which provide the information for the aiming, are very special. They are the only eyes in the animal kingdom with both a 360-degree view and three-dimensional vision. The

Pardalis chameleons' color patterns look similar, but each is unique—much like our fingerprints.

area that picks out colors and brings images into sharp focus is four times more sensitive than the one in our own eyes.

The bulging eyes are covered with flexible skin that is formed from a joined upper and lower eyelid. There is a small peephole that exposes only the pupil and the red or yellow iris. To look around, the chameleon must move its entire eye. If it moved only the eyeball, its eyelid would block the view.

The only time a chameleon's eyes are still is when they are shut at night and the few seconds before the tongue is launched, when they are fixed on the next meal. When the animal is awake, the eyes are constantly moving, searching for danger or looking for prey. Perhaps the most remarkable thing about the chameleon's eyes is the fact that they move independently. Most of the time, a chameleon receives two very

The tail hooks around a branch whenever the tongue goes into action, as with this brevicornus zeroing in on a tasty bug.

different images of its world. One eye may be checking the sky for birds of prey while the other eye scans the rain forest for snakes, big spiders, or other chameleon killers that creep up from below. Scientists don't know how the chameleon's tiny brain edits together the two different pictures from its rotating eyes.

The chameleon's super sight has taken a lot of the brain space that is usually given to the other senses. Chameleons have been shortchanged in hearing ability. They are almost deaf. For me, one of the best things about chameleon study is that I don't have to be quiet! They can't hear me coming no matter how much noise I make crashing through the jungle. Chameleons have no outer ear—nothing is visible, not even the tiniest of holes. Scientists think that chameleons can hear a few sounds, though— low-pitched ones such as the muffled wing beats of hawks or eagles or the rasping of a snake's scales. These sounds, too low in pitch for easy detection by a human ear, are the most important in a chameleon's world.

"Chameleons stink," Tara cried while she was shooting a close-up photograph of a pardalis. I thought something had happened to make her dislike chameleons. Perhaps one of the grumpy creatures had bitten her. "Don't forget how beautiful they are," I called. She laughed, and answered, "This one looks beautiful all right, but he doesn't smell beautiful. He stinks like rotten meat." He did, too. After investigating, we discovered the source of the foul smell. Glands near the pardalis' mouth were oozing a stinky solution used to attract flies.

Chameleons make use of sweet smells, although they don't produce them. By hiding in bushes with flowers that attract insects, the chameleon increases its chances of catching a meal. It's a good strategy, but it can backfire on a young chameleon that doesn't know that some flower-loving insects can sting. A young pardalis of our acquaintance learned about bees—the hard way. He zapped a bee, and it did what bees do when they're attacked. It stung. The chameleon obviously felt the sting, because his calm green-and-blue pattern darkened to an angry black as he ate his spicy meal. Not all chameleons have this reaction to bees. Bearded chameleons eat almost nothing but bees. Pardalis regularly eat venomous creatures such as spiders and scorpions. How they avoid getting sick is one of the things we don't know about chameleons.

The chameleon sits totally motionless for hours, waiting for food to come within range of its sharpshooting tongue. The ability to remain still is one of the reasons chameleons are such successful insect hunters. Insects have flicker vision. Their compound eyes can't see stationary objects very well.

After a tasty insect or other snack, a chameleon must make sure it stays warm. Body processes like digestion need heat. If a chameleon remains cold after eating, food will rot in its stomach and it might die.

A drab female pardalis shows the sexual dimorphism (difference in form—in the case of pardalis, color and size—between males and females) of her species.

Wise men are like the chameleon: They keep one eye on the past and one eye on the future. —old Malagasy saying

The Vanishing Act 5

In the southern skies there is a constellation of sixteen stars called Chameleon. It would be almost impossible to draw a picture of it. Like the earthly chameleons for which it was named, the star cluster looks different every time you see it. Some of its stars are pulsars that fade in and out. The rest keep eclipsing each other in a heavenly vanishing act.

On Earth, chameleons are doing their own vanishing act. The people of Madagascar think they are ghosts. They are so afraid of the harmless little creatures that many kill them on sight. In some places people not only believe chameleons are spirits of the dead, they think they are poisonous (which they are not).

The fate of chameleons is tied to that of their home. If the tropical forests disappear, so will many, perhaps most, of the chameleons. Right now it seems likely that will happen. Tropical forests everywhere are threatened, especially those in Madagascar, where many of the chameleons are found.

People have taken over and changed the spaces chameleons need to live in. Some, like the pardalis, are thriving in the changed habitat. Others, like minima and parsonii, aren't. Many species may become extinct without our even knowing they existed.

These reptiles are important and should be saved. Chameleons eat insects—carriers of disease and man's main competitors for food. Without insect eaters, the rain forests

and possibly the entire world would be overrun with bugs!

There is an old Malagasy saying: *Wise men are like the chameleon: They keep one eye on the past and one eye on the future.* The many people who are breeding chameleons in captivity and preserving wild places for them are doing just that. To save the chameleons, we need to know more about them. There is much work for young scientists who want to make sure there will always be a "rainbow" in the rain forest.

Chameleon Facts

Common name: Chameleon (kuh-MEEL-yun). No special name for males, females, or babies.

Scientific names: Chamaeleonidae (family). Pardalis: Chamaeleo pardalis. Parsonii: Chamaeleo parsonii. Minima: Brookesia minima

Number of species: Species number varies due to differing methods of classification. There are about 128 distinct species. Additional undescribed species are thought to exist.

Size: Males are larger than females in most egg-laying species; females are the same size or larger in live-bearing species. Smallest: minima (one inch long). Largest: parsonii (over two feet long). Chamaeleo oustaleti, although not as heavy, are as long as parsonii. Pardalis reach one and a half feet in length.

Color: Each species has its own range, but green and brown predominate.

Behavior: Slow moving, secretive, solitary, aggressive, and territorial

Range/Habitat: Africa, Madagascar, Middle East, western India (one species), and southern Europe (one species). All ecosystems, ranging from rain forest to desert to mountains

Food: Insects; small birds, mammals, and lizards

Predators: Humans, large birds, snakes, spiders, lizards, and lemurs (Madagascar only)

Life span: Unknown in the wild, but thought to average two years with some individuals living up to six years. In captivity, up to twelve years

Reproduction: Some species lay eggs and others have live babies. Gestation or incubation ranges from three to eighteen months. Some species can produce several hundred offspring in a year.

Population: Unknown. Some species common; others endangered

Index

(Entries in italics refer to photos and captions.)